# STAND FOR THE TRUTH

**PETER MASTERS**

SWORD & TROWEL
METROPOLITAN TABERNACLE
LONDON

# STAND FOR THE TRUTH
(formerly Separation & Obedience)

© Peter Masters 1983
This revised booklet edition first published 1996
Reprinted 2003

SWORD & TROWEL
Metropolitan Tabernacle
Elephant & Castle
London SE1 6SD

ISBN 1 899046 11 9

Cover design by Andrew Sides

*All rights reserved. No part of this publication may be reproduced or transmitted in any form or by any means, electronic or mechanical, including photocopy, recording, or any information storage and retrieval system, without permission in writing from the publisher.*

Printed in Oradea, Romania by RomFlair Press S.L.R.

# Stand for the Truth

## A new scene for Bible-believers

ARE WE AWARE that many Bible-believers now hold views which are unprecedented in evangelical history? Readers who have come into the faith since the 1950s may not realise just how much the present evangelical scene has moved from its traditional moorings. For most of church history, born-again people have zealously guarded the fundamental principles of the Gospel. They have maintained a clear and distinctive witness, refusing to endorse or commend those who teach 'another gospel'. The evangelical tradition is a courageous story of loyalty to the Truth.

Throughout the dark ages, successive groups of 'separatists' held aloft the light of the Gospel in the face of unrelenting persecution from the Roman Catholic Church. The Reformation is the story of Martin Luther's heroic stand for the soul-saving doctrines of the Bible. Following Luther, was a 'noble army of martyrs', ready to defend those doctrines with their lives.

After these came the Mayflower pilgrims, the puritans, nonconformists, and so many others who loved the Lord and His Word more than their own comforts, and contended for 'the faith which was once delivered unto the saints'.

When the Oxford Movement arose in the nineteenth century, spreading Catholicism in the Church of England, evangelicals rallied as one to the defence of the Gospel. Then, as another great attack on biblical faith reached its zenith in the early 1900s, a massive response was mounted by the well-known names of evangelicalism of America and Britain, leading to a famous publication (then possessed by virtually all evangelical pastors) – *The Fundamentals*. We make mention of these things only to show that in the past evangelicals were always great contenders for the Gospel. Traditional, orthodox evangelicalism never sold the pass. Indeed, were the stalwarts of the past to reappear among us today, they would be appalled at what is now being done by many evangelicals. Those of us who sound the alarm today are not a maverick fringe. We stand four-square where evangelicals always stood until quite recently.

Today, however, numerous evangelicals are willing to surrender the vital heart of the faith. They have been persuaded to adopt a much vaguer definition of what it means to be 'saved', and to think that evangelical conversion is not absolutely necessary. They have been persuaded that Catholics and theological liberals – who deny the inerrancy of Scripture, and fundamental doctrines such as the atonement – are truly saved no matter what they believe. Never before have evangelicals been so ready to blur the line between saved and unsaved, true and false. Where do we stand on these matters? Are they of concern to us?

The new attitude of compromise may be illustrated from any number of evangelical conferences, events and publications throughout the world. We select only three examples, one from the USA and two from Britain. In March 1994, in the USA, a number of leading evangelicals in co-operation with leading Catholics published a challenge to all Christians entitled, *Evangelicals and Catholics Together*. This asserted that evangelicals and Catholics are equally saved in God's sight, and should stop evangelising one another, and work together for the kingdom of God. Without any qualification or reservation, the document insisted that all 'evangelicals and Catholics are brothers and sisters in Christ.' In other words, people may be truly saved without having the slightest notion of justification by faith alone. The evangelical authors of this challenge included some of the best-known names in the evangelical world from charismatic to reformed. As far as these leaders were concerned, the Reformation was all a tragic mistake.

In Britain, the same kind of view began to be expressed among evangelical clergy in the Church of England as long ago as the 1960s. At a major conference (held at Keele, in 1967) the majority of evangelical clergy decided they would no longer view the Church of England as a largely apostate body, or disown its Anglo-Catholic and liberal wings. They promised to adopt a new attitude in which they would regard the *whole* Church of England as a valid church in the sight of God. They would no longer see themselves as being the sole possessors of spiritual life and Truth. Non-evangelical teaching would, in future, be respected as truly Christian.

Ten years later evangelical Anglicans held another conference (at Nottingham) where they drew up *The Nottingham Statement*.[*] This declared that all Roman Catholics were true Christians, saying – 'Seeing ourselves and Roman Catholics as fellow Christians, we repent of attitudes that have seemed to deny it.' Catholics were said to be 'saved' in the fullest sense, even though they lacked any testimony of evangelical conversion. (Elsewhere the *Nottingham Statement* conceded that it might be possible for people to be saved through other religions, without hearing the name of Christ.)

This same *Statement* (representing the views of the vast majority of evangelical Anglican clergy) affirmed that unity with the Catholic Church was the desire and goal of evangelical Anglicans. In 1977, therefore, evangelical Anglicans publicly denied and disowned the

---

[*]The Chairman of the Nottingham Conference was the leading figure among evangelical Anglicans, Dr John R. W. Stott.

*exclusive* status of the Gospel as the *only* way of salvation. The Catholic way and the liberal way could also save.

Evangelical Anglicans were not alone in adopting these views, for evangelicals in other denominations were moving along the same lines. What are we to make of this change in position on the part of professedly Bible-believing pastors? How can leading ministers claim to believe in evangelical conversion for themselves, and at the same time say that those who reject the biblical way are also 'saved', regardless of what they believe? Why have these evangelical brethren decided to go comprehensive in their doctrinal views? Why have they chosen to turn away from the biblical commands to maintain a distinctive testimony, separate from false teaching?

## *A biblical perspective*

In the opening chapters of the Bible we are told how Satan undermined God's instruction to Adam and Eve to leave well alone the fruit of one particular tree. The tempter said to Eve – 'Yea, hath God said, Ye shall not eat of every tree of the garden?' *(Genesis 3.1.)* To this day Satan casts doubt on God's command to leave certain things alone. When God says, 'Remain separate from false religion and worldliness,' the devil whispers, 'Has God really said that?'

It is no exaggeration to say that most of the Bible concentrates on this one particular stratagem of Satan. The Pentateuch constantly focuses attention on the refusal of God's people to leave alone those things which God had forbidden them to touch. All their troubles sprang from their attempts to combine Truth and falsehood, pure worship and false worship. When God commanded them to leave the Canaanites alone, they intermarried with them, polluting the true faith with idolatrous worship. The *Book of Judges* records cycles of prosperity and blessing followed by seasons of oppression and despair. What was the problem? Every time it was idolatry. They mixed the true faith with false gods, involving themselves with forbidden things.

From the time of Samuel to that of Nehemiah we may trace the same problem of compromise, namely, confederacy with God's enemies, intermarriage, and so forth. Old Testament history is a tragic tale of forbidden alliances. The chief cry from the hearts of the prophets was a warning against compromise with forbidden things.

Every believer in the Christian dispensation has heard the familiar voice of the enemy, in connection with some forbidden fruit, whisper, 'Has God really said you may not have that? Think what you will gain if you are broad-minded about this.'

When it comes to separation from false teaching the devil says, 'Has God really issued a command not to worship, evangelise or study theology with non-evangelicals? You will not come to grief. You will prosper and your testimony will flourish by making the most of the advantages offered. You will get opportunities which you will never have by standing apart. Is it good to be negative and to sit in judgement upon others? Is salvation really limited to those with an evangelical experience of the new birth? Is it necessary to expose Catholic doctrine as wrong, and liberalism as a lie? Can we not see good in these things and co-operate with these people? Surely it is a terrible thing to bring division among God's people. How can anyone be so arrogant as to claim a monopoly of the Truth?'

The devil hates the biblical doctrine of separation from false teaching, because he is the father of lies and the author of confusion. The tragedy of modern evangelicalism is that discernment and distinctiveness have largely been abandoned, giving Satan a free hand to do his worst. The issue before us is whether, as individuals or as churches, we will listen to God when He commands us to maintain a distinctive evangelical testimony, and to leave false teachers alone. Should we serve in apostate, Gospel-denying denominations? Should we participate in ecumenical campaigns and ventures? Should we give recognition, fellowship and support to non-evangelicals? This booklet is about love and loyalty to the way of salvation revealed in the Bible. It is about the positive virtue of separation from false teaching. It is about taking a traditional evangelical stand for the Truth.

## *The biblical command to be distinct and separate as evangelicals*

The Word of God teaches that Christians must keep themselves apart from any form of religion which contradicts and undermines the central, soul-saving doctrines of the Christian faith. This is a primary and binding command found in many passages, none of which are in the slightest degree unclear or controversial. We shall look just briefly at ten of these.

First, the command to be a distinctive and separate people is plainly stated in *2 Corinthians 6.14-17* –

'Be ye not equally yoked together with unbelievers: for what fellowship hath righteousness with unrighteousness? and what communion hath light with darkness? and what concord hath Christ with Belial? or what part hath he that believeth with an infidel? and what agreement hath the temple of God with idols? for ye are the temple of the living God; as God hath said, I will dwell in them, and walk in them; and I will be their God, and they shall be my people. Wherefore come out from among them, and be ye separate, saith the Lord.'

The Greek word translated 'separate' refers to the setting of a boundary. (The word 'horizon' comes directly from this Greek word.) Paul tells us that we are to be separate in the sense that a boundary is set, which must never be crossed. The false teachers and their errors must be *out of bounds* to us, or *beyond the horizon*. We must never have fellowship with them at any level. The apostle uses the strongest available words to command us never to be in fellowship with religious teachers who deny the Word of God and uphold false doctrine.

We must certainly never be 'yoked' together, which means that we must never work with false religious teachers in joint spiritual ventures of any kind. We must never be found on the same team of oxen. We are forbidden by this command to sit on committees, share platforms or serve on pastoral teams with such teachers. Equally we are told never to join in church assemblies and denominations with them.* The 'yoke' is the bond of service. As far as God is concerned, false teachers who deny the fundamentals of the faith must never be given spiritual recognition, nor may we recognise their churches as valid churches in the sight of God.

We must certainly have pity and concern for all who are ensnared in error. Jude warns believers about false Christians, pointing out that some may be saveable. Save such, he says, with fear, 'pulling them out of the fire; hating even the garment spotted by the flesh' *(Jude 23)*. The rule of Scripture is that we reach out to non-evangelical 'Christians' as *outsiders*, but that we never do or say anything which would condone, flatter, dignify or recognise their false teaching.

Our second text commanding a distinctive evangelical testimony, and separation from error, is *Romans 16.17*. Here Paul commands that churches should – 'mark them which cause divisions and offences contrary to the doctrine which ye have learned; and avoid them.' This verse refers to all false teachers who cause people to miss the Truth. It applies today to the Roman Catholic Church, which veered away from biblical Christianity many centuries ago, and has grown to vast proportions, teaching the exact opposite of the salvation doctrines given in the Bible. The text also refers to theological liberals, who deny the inspiration and infallibility of the Bible, and who sneer at most fundamental doctrines of the faith. They deny the

---

*The main denominations have declined into theological liberalism over a period of 140 years. For many years numerous evangelicals stayed within these and fought to regain them to the Truth. They stood firmly against the non-evangelicals. The writer of these pages does not wish to criticise evangelicals who have earnestly contended for the faith within spiritually decadent denominations. He believes they ought to have left, but acknowledges the courageous efforts of many who have fought from within. The chief problem today is that most evangelicals who remain within the old denominations have stopped contending and begun to compromise. Most now accept the non-evangelical element as legitimate and equally Christian.

existence of hell, and teach that all mankind will be eternally safe. Both movements beguile the souls of millions of people. It is no wonder the apostle denounces such teachers and movements. They are so offensive to God and dangerous to souls that they must never be recognised or associated with.

Is this command obeyed when evangelists invite non-evangelicals to participate in their meetings? Is it obeyed when they send converts to Catholic and other non-evangelical churches to be instructed by them? Is it obeyed by evangelical ministers who work closely with non-evangelicals in denominations, sitting on committees and sharing intimately in various church activities?

Our third text commanding separation is *1 Corinthians 5.9-13* where the apostle commands believers 'not to keep company' with professing Christians guilty of particular sins. Although he refers mainly to personal sins, he twice mentions *idolatry*, the main religious compromise of those days. There is to be no fellowship with the person who claims to be Christian, yet who continues to practise idolatry. We are not even to eat with such a person (when to eat is an expression of acceptance and fellowship). This is the Lord's command, given through Paul, concerning those who claim to be Christian, but who practise false religion. False teachers are 'the enemies of the cross of Christ', as Paul says in *Philippians 3.18*. Believers must never fraternise and identify with them in a way which would endorse their views and their spiritual standing.

Our fourth text commanding a distinctive, separate evangelical stand is *Galatians 1.8*, where the apostle Paul warns that false teachers may come equipped with great gifts and highly attractive personalities. They may possess gracious, loving ways and considerable charm, but if they represent false teaching (as non-evangelicals do) then true believers must not extend fellowship to them. Says Paul – 'But though we, or an angel from heaven, preach any other gospel unto you than that which we have preached unto you, let him be accursed.' The word *accursed* means that a person is to be banned or excommunicated, and treated as utterly unacceptable. False teaching is so destructive to souls, and so offensive to God, that Paul says that if he himself or any member of his party were to preach a different Gospel, he was to be *accursed.*

This command is so important that the apostle is moved by the Spirit to repeat himself, and in *Galatians 1.9* he says, 'As we said before, so say I now again, If any man preach any other gospel unto you than that ye have received, let him be accursed.' He is to be treated as a total outsider. Is this clear command obeyed today when evangelical leaders issue statements declaring that all Catholic clergy (though they teach justification by works and encourage the worship of Mary) are to be accepted as true Christians? Is this command obeyed when theological liberals (who reject the Bible, the atonement, the need for conversion, and other vital truths also) are embraced as true Christians?

Our fifth text is *2 John 6-11,* where John, the disciple of love, is used by the Holy Spirit to give one of the clearest commands about separation in the entire Bible, instructing us not to fellowship with false teachers under any circumstances. He begins by reminding us that love for the Lord is shown in obedience and faithfulness to His revealed Word. He then proceeds to say that many deceivers have come, 'who confess not that Jesus Christ is come in the flesh. This is a deceiver and an antichrist ... Whosoever transgresseth, and abideth not in the doctrine of Christ, hath not God ... If there come any unto you, and bring not this doctrine, receive him not into your house, neither bid him God speed' *(2 John 7-10).*

We are taught that any Christian teacher who does not truly believe in Christ as the incarnate Saviour, is devoid of any personal relationship with God. If such a person comes among us, he is not to be given fellowship or recognition, nor is he to be even greeted in the name of Christ.

But to whom does this apply? Does it apply only to those who openly deny that the Saviour came in the flesh? If this is the case, then Catholics and many other non-evangelicals would be eligible for fellowship, because although they deny evangelical conversion, they do affirm that Jesus Christ came in the flesh. This is exactly how today's compromising evangelicals interpret the passage. They say that Catholics and even many liberals qualify for fellowship (in other words, they are truly saved) because they believe that Christ came in the flesh. However, it should be obvious that this interpretation is absurdly shallow, stripping the text of its full meaning. Will people, at death, be admitted to Heaven even though they were never saved, and though they rejected most of the Gospel, merely because they believed in the incarnation?

To confess that Jesus Christ came in the flesh is not merely a technical assent to the incarnation. It means that we act upon that belief, believing *all* the Saviour's teaching, and acting upon His commands. If we *really* believe He is God, then we will surely believe all that He said about Himself, and about His work on Calvary for the salvation of sinners. We will obey His call to repent and be converted. We will readily accept and believe the soul-saving doctrines of the Gospel. Yet these things have been denied and attacked with great ferocity by the Roman Catholic Church, and by other non-evangelicals. It is obvious that they do not *truly* and *deeply* believe that Jesus Christ came in the flesh, because they do not respect Him enough to obey His teaching.

The words of *2 John 7-10* call us to refuse recognition to religious teachers who do not respect, accept and obey the words and actions of the incarnate Son of God. Catholics and liberals have substituted human ideas and ceremonies for the teaching of the Lord, and in so doing they have rejected His authority.

Our sixth text commanding separation from false teaching is *1 Timothy 4.1* and *7*, where we are told that all false teaching is the work of the devil and his demons. 'Now the Spirit speaketh expressly, that in the latter times some shall depart from the faith, giving heed to seducing spirits, and doctrines of devils.' One of the chief tasks of the devil's host today is to lure and tempt people into false doctrine. On no account must we recognise or co-operate with those who are the propagators of the doctrines of demons. 'Refuse profane and old wives' fables,' says Paul. Timothy is to reject all that comes from sources other than the Word of God. From the beginning of the epistle he is charged with silencing (in the church) the teaching of any other doctrine *(1 Timothy 1.3-4)*. Today, however, many evangelicals are saying that the doctrines of Rome and of the liberals are equally effective to bring people to salvation. This is an astounding development for evangelicalism. To give recognition to such doctrines is to give aid to the work of demons.

In *1 Timothy 4.2*, Paul says that many of those who teach against God's revealed Truth speak 'lies in hypocrisy'. Apparently they *know* what they are doing. They know that there is no real power and truth in the things that they say. Many know they are manipulators of Truth. They are not sincere in their views.

Our seventh text is *1 Timothy 6.3-5*, where Paul again commands that we withdraw from those who do not teach the words and doctrine of our Lord. 'If any man teach otherwise, and consent not to wholesome words, even the words of our Lord Jesus Christ, and to the doctrine which is according to godliness . . . from such withdraw thyself.' By now it should be clear that the documents referred to earlier in this booklet – *Evangelicals and Catholics Together*, and *The Nottingham Statement* – are written in head-on defiance of the plain commands of God's Word. They represent glaring compromise.

Our eighth text is *2 Timothy 2.16-21*, where Paul commands us to 'shun profane and vain babblings: for they will increase unto more ungodliness.' 'Shun' means to turn away, and avoid. This is a duty. There is to be no spiritual recognition of false teachers, and no fellowship. In this passage, Paul pictures the professing church as containing many people devoid of value. These are the false teachers and their disciples. He then says, 'If a man therefore purge himself from these, he shall be a vessel unto honour, sanctified, and meet for the master's use, and prepared unto every good work.' 'Purge' means to cleanse thoroughly. True churches and true believers must be completely untainted by teaching which contradicts the soul-saving doctrines of the Gospel.

Our ninth text is *2 Timothy 3.5*, in which Paul refers to some people – 'Having a form of godliness, but denying the power thereof: from such turn away.' Catholics and liberals deny the powerful, transforming work of God in conversion as an instantaneous experience, received immediately in response to repentance and faith. We cannot and must not compromise such vital doctrine. We must 'turn away' from such teachers.

Our tenth text is *Ephesians 5.11*, where Paul says: 'Have no fellowship with the unfruitful works of darkness, but rather reprove them.' This text covers both moral and doctrinal matters. It is a fundamental principle taught throughout the Bible. God's Truth must be preserved. We must plainly show the errors of false doctrines, lest people should be led astray.

From such texts as these it should be apparent that it is disobedience of the most serious kind to give spiritual recognition to those who teach another 'gospel'. We may show love to people who are in error by trying to win them to the Truth. We may have sympathy for them in their darkness, and we may endeavour to reach them *as outsiders*, but we must never condone and recognise their teaching, for this is a high crime against the Word of God. The Lord commands His people to have no fellowship with false teachers. Is any reader involved in any alliance through which he or she identifies with false teachers, giving them recognition and encouragement? Separation from false teachers is not an idea of men, it is what our Lord requires of us, and if we are true to Him we must obey Him.

## *Separation is positive – not negative*

The biblical command to maintain a distinctive evangelical witness, and to keep apart from false teaching, should not be regarded as a negative matter, because it is one of the most positive and protective aspects of Christian obedience. Biblical separation may be defined as obedience to the great 'leave alone' texts of Scripture. It is positive because it safeguards the doctrinal and spiritual purity of the churches, and their effectiveness in spreading the Gospel of Christ. Separation may be seen in a more positive light by considering a number of 'equivalent' terms. Separation is, for example, a form of *devotedness*, because it speaks of our being exclusively committed to the Gospel of Christ. *Separation* means that we are exclusively on the Lord's side and that we render no service whatever to His enemies. The word *devotion* conveys a beautiful and positive fidelity to the Lord and this is exactly what separation really implies.

Other equivalent terms would include *committedness, loyalty, faithfulness* and *genuineness*. All these words show the positive and wholesome nature of true separation. They speak of love for the Lord, and readiness to serve Him and Him only, no matter what the cost. Separation bids us keep away from the things He hates and remain faithful to Him no matter what overtures or advances false teachers may make to us.

The separation command of *2 Corinthians 6* concludes with this gracious promise (vv 17-18) – 'And I will receive you, and will be a Father unto you, and ye shall be my sons and daughters, saith the Lord Almighty.' Separation is positive because it is a means to a great end; a road to a great destination; a duty resulting in a glorious blessing. The Lord says, in effect, to evangelicals who dabble with wrong alliances: 'I want to receive you, I want to have you exclusively. I am embarrassed by your alliances. I cannot move among you and bless you as I would. I cannot make My presence manifest among you. I long to touch your congregations and bless all your families in a mighty way. You pay homage to those who are My enemies and you look for help from those who hate My Word. You play the music of a fallen world and smile upon those who are worldly. You have embarrassed Me out of My own churches and grieved away My Spirit. I want to love you and embrace you and move among you but I cannot do so in any great way until you separate from the things which are offensive to Me. When you truly show your love for Me, then I will come to you.'

How can we work and co-operate with those who scorn the Word and spurn the sufficiency of Calvary? Separation from error is an essential act of true commitment and loyalty to the Lord and His Word, and it is the positive path to blessing.

## *Secondary separation*

Clearly we should remain separate from non-evangelicals. But should we also separate from fellow *evangelicals* who wilfully and enthusiastically fellowship and co-operate with non-evangelicals? Should we hold ourselves apart from those evangelicals who now give full recognition to Catholics and theological liberals? Should we break fellowship with the former as well as the latter? This is what has become known as 'secondary separation'. Is this right or wrong? The answer becomes clear once we appreciate the *strength* of the command to keep strictly apart from all false religion. It is an imperative, vital and *primary* command, not a piece of optional advice on some matter of relatively minor significance. It is binding upon all Christians. Furthermore, the Bible teaches that believers who refuse point-blank to obey this command become helpers and participants with false teachers in their evil work. They may not realise or accept this, but the Bible warns them that it is nevertheless true. They help the cause of error, and therefore place themselves under the censure of the Lord, and under the rule of separation which must be applied by all Christians loyal to the Lord's will.

*2 John 9-11* is emphatic on this matter: 'Whosoever transgresseth, and abideth not in the doctrine of Christ, hath not God... If there come any unto you, and bring not this doctrine, receive him not into your house, neither bid him God speed: FOR HE THAT BIDDETH HIM GOD SPEED IS PARTAKER OF HIS EVIL DEEDS.' When professing evangelicals (especially leaders) disobey the command of God to maintain a distinctive testimony, unassociated with false teachers, they participate in the evil deeds of the latter in at least four different ways:

(1) Non-separators deal a terrible blow to the exclusive nature of the message of the Gospel. When evangelicals are seen to accommodate the viewpoint of non-evangelicals and to accept their claims to spiritual life, the clear teaching of the Word is undermined. The line between Truth and error becomes blurred, and also the distinction between saved and unsaved. Believers who look on are liable to stop thinking of 'conversion' in precise, evangelical terms.

(2) Non-separators help the devil to achieve one of his main objectives – to cause such confusion that the world no longer sees a distinctive, biblical Christian community standing clearly apart from Catholic and liberal error. Non-separating evangelicals communicate to the world the idea that all so-called Christian churches are the same. Nothing is more crippling to the true testimony of evangelicalism. In the nineteenth century even unsaved people knew the Protestant arguments against Catholic dogma. But today (through compromise) evangelicals have long since surrendered any distinctive place in the general knowledge of the public.

(3) Non-separators lower the guard of the people of God, exposing them to infiltration by false believers and false doctrine. Once the people follow the example of their non-separating ministers, learning to tolerate and accept 'other views', then the way is prepared for a major doctrinal collapse. Non-evangelicals could never penetrate evangelical churches without 'inside help'. They need a 'pass' into the household of God, which only an evangelical 'collaborator' can give them, as he extends to them credibility, recognition and opportunity.

(4) Non-separators encourage false teachers in their infidelity and sin, and so strengthen them in their work. The rise of theological liberalism in the denominations, and its take-over of them, was funded almost entirely by evangelicals. When these opponents of the Gospel first infiltrated colleges and publishing institutions, non-separating evangelicals continued to pay the bills and support them. Almost all the present-day liberal theological colleges and churches in the historic denominations were originally built by the blood,

sweat and toil of evangelicals. Then, a subsequent generation of non-separating evangelicals gave them away! This continues today in denominations where evangelicals give their money to support home and overseas missions mainly staffed and run by non-evangelicals. Not only do non-separating evangelicals support false teachers at a practical level, but they also seal them in their spiritual delusion by failing to challenge them about their lost spiritual condition.

These are the tragic consequences of disobedience to God. Satan rejoices, the Holy Spirit is grieved, and the cause of Christ is seriously wounded. If the non-separators are ministers, their flocks see a major area of biblical teaching set aside by their spiritual leaders, and thus the authority of the Bible is further undermined. The words of *2 John 11* condemn compromise. They indicate that the person who places himself on the side of the enemy must be regarded as guilty of a grievous sin against the Lord and His work. The non-separator makes himself a sharer of the damage done by the false teacher. Without doubt there is guilt by association.

The duty of secondary separation (withdrawing fellowship and co-operation from evangelicals, especially leaders, who wilfully support non-evangelicals) is also affirmed in *2 Thessalonians 3.6, 14 and 15*, where the apostle shows that wilful rejection of *any* of the fundamental duties of the Christian life *must* meet with the strictures of church discipline and separation. The vital verse reads: 'Now we command you, brethren, in the name of our Lord Jesus Christ, that ye withdraw yourselves from every brother that walketh disorderly,* and not after the tradition which he received of us.'

The 'tradition' consists of all the fundamental doctrines and duties which the inspired apostles taught. It includes the crucial commands to keep apart from false religion. Anyone who is unruly, and who flagrantly ignores these apostolic instructions, is to be warned and, if unrepentant, to be 'withdrawn from'.

In *2 Thessalonians 3* Paul applies this principle particularly to loafers and busybodies, but this is only one application of a vital part of church discipline. (If a person must be disciplined for laziness or sponging off others, how much more must he be disciplined for spurning the command to separate from false teaching.)

This New Testament insistence that believers should not compromise with God's enemies is also seen in the Old Testament. In *2 Chronicles 19.2* God speaks through Jehu the prophet to rebuke godly King Jehoshaphat of Judah for making an alliance with Ahab, king of Israel. When Jehoshaphat was asked by Ahab to help him in war, he replied – 'I am as thou art, and my people as thy people; and we will be with thee in the war' *(2 Chronicles 18.3)*. This is exactly the stance taken by ecumenical evangelicals today in their relationships with non-evangelicals. But God condemned Jehoshaphat, saying – 'Shouldest thou help the ungodly, and love them that hate the Lord? therefore is wrath upon thee from before the Lord.'

Even though Jehoshaphat later reformed his conduct, yet his friendship and alliance with Ahab cost him the loss of all his children by the hand of his eldest son, and the eventual execution of all his grandchildren. The principle was made painfully clear that when God's people compromise with the Lord's enemies, they commit serious sin, and trouble results.

Failure to remain separate from non-evangelicals and their teaching is disobedience to God, and it incurs great guilt. This is affirmed once again in *Revelation 18.4-5*, where the corruption and fornication of Babylon is described. We read – 'And I heard another voice

---

*The *NIV* has paraphrased the Greek in rendering the passage – 'We command you, brothers, to keep away from every brother who is *idle*...' However, the Greek word is correctly translated *disorderly* (as in the *AV*) or *unruly* (as in the *NASB*). It means – out of order, insubordinate, unruly, lawless, or undisciplined. It means 'walking out of step' *(MLB)*. One of the forms which disorderliness takes is *idleness*, but the word includes all forms of disorderliness and it is quite wrong to limit the meaning as the *NIV*, and also the *RSV*, does.

The Greek for *idle* is quite different, and Paul uses this elsewhere. If he had meant to use it here he would have done so. In substituting *idle* for *disorderly* the *NIV* and *RSV* have obscured the vital principle, namely, that wilful rejection of God's order is an offence attracting church discipline. The errant translations have turned the entire passage into a comment on one particular application of the principle, namely – the problem of malingerers.

from heaven, saying, Come out of her, my people, that ye be not partakers of her sins, and that ye receive not of her plagues. For her sins have reached unto heaven, and God hath remembered her iniquities.' Some say that Babylon represents the Church of Rome. Others say she represents sinful society in all ages. Either way the central message is the same. If Christian people make alliances with those who are the Lord's enemies, they participate in their sins, become infected by their diseases, and place themselves under God's discipline.

Compromising evangelicals may not *intend* to encourage Christ's enemies, but they most certainly do, because the Lord says so. When God forbids these alliances His children must not overrule or ignore Him. Evangelicals who co-operate with false teachers are definitely guilty of a terrible wrong, as Scripture repeatedly asserts. Other believers cannot, therefore, walk in close fellowship or co-operation with them. They are disobedient to the Lord in a vital matter.

Some have said that they cannot accept any idea of secondary separation because it would lead to a third and fourth stage. They say they would be obliged to separate from evangelicals who fail to separate from evangelicals who fail to separate from non-evangelicals. And so it would go on. But this is a foolish reason for neglecting the command of Scripture. We do not usually set aside a command of Scripture because we are afraid of taking matters to an extreme. Those who scorn secondary separation only show that they are reluctant to separate at all. In his famous sermon 'No Compromise', C. H. Spurgeon offered these words: 'That I might not stultify my testimony I have cut myself clear of those who err from the faith, and even from those who associate with them' (*Metropolitan Tabernacle Pulpit* 1888, No. 2047).

## *'And of some have compassion, making a difference'*

Obviously, when we speak of withdrawing fellowship from other evangelicals who co-operate and fellowship with false teachers, we must not forget that some may be ignorant of God's commands, or unaware of their situation. We must possess a sincere and sympathetic concern to 'win' them before we think of separating.

Numerous evangelicals have been wrongly led by others into identifying with non-evangelicals. They need biblical light on the matter. Most truly born-again people are instinctively uneasy about compromise, but they may have been encouraged into error by ministers whom they trusted. Many evangelicals are not deeply aware of the extent to which their ministers or their denominations have compromised. We may have the task of helping such believers to see the reality, and of sensitively urging them to face the issue.

We may know ministers in compromised situations who are only just beginning to think about their positions. Or we may know ministers who have long held pastoral charge in a liberal denomination, but they minister in relatively isolated places, far removed from direct contact with their denominational apostasy. We must be careful not to disapprove of people without an appreciation of their circumstances. We must always be anxious to reach, help and win over other evangelicals as they face these issues.

However, in these tragic days there are also deliberately and deeply compromised ministers and clergymen who have had ample opportunity to see the issues. They have been pleaded and remonstrated with about their compromise. But despite all such efforts, they remain indifferent to the clear commands of the Lord. They seem wilfully determined to disobey Him and to encourage their congregations to do the same. In the case of such men, there can be no question that we should separate from them in obedience to *2 Thessalonians 3*, and pray that they, by God's grace, may become ashamed of what they are doing. In secondary separation, it should be emphasised that we have in mind *obdurate* people who have rejected the Lord's command.

To return to *2 Thessalonians 3.14,* the apostle commands us – 'And if any man obey not our word by this epistle, note that man, and have no company with him, that he may be ashamed.' How is this to be done? Paul proceeds in these words: 'Yet count him not as an enemy, but admonish him as a brother.' The assumption is that the disorderly person is a true evangelical. Does this modify the level of separation? Not at all, for to 'have no company' with someone is not something which may be implemented in different degrees. It must always mean a clean break. However, because the offender is a professing evangelical we have a duty to do something *in addition* to separating. We are to admonish the person. Paul's words do not mean that *officially* we separate, but *unofficially* we continue to have close relations. He does not suggest that we distinguish between public fellowship and private fellowship. His words mean that we cease all co-operation and fellowship, but take whatever opportunity may arise to warn the offender of the error of his ways. We couple our separation with admonition.

The discipline of the Bible is designed both to protect the Truth and also, if possible, to reform those who can be turned back from their error. If all loyal evangelicals obeyed the Scripture and had no company with their brethren who committed compromise, the latter might soon become ashamed and change their ways. But compromisers often continue to enjoy considerable cordiality and approval from the Bible-believing community. If they are writers, their books are warmly reviewed and their views continually quoted. Is it likely that they will ever become ashamed of their conduct?

It should not be necessary to add that before any secondary separation takes place, a space of time must be allowed for those who err to change their minds, just as the Lord gave the offending churches of Asia a space of time to repent.

## *Arguments against separation from error*

Many sincere Christians have been persuaded to reject separation on the grounds stated in the following pages. These ten arguments are those which are heard most often. Our reply, with scriptural support, is given in each case.

## (1) Joining hands with non-evangelicals gets opportunities for the Gospel

'There can be nothing wrong with co-operating with non-evangelicals in evangelistic endeavours and in doctrinally-mixed denominations when these create opportunities for the Gospel. If the evangelist can get a larger crowd by joining forces with modernists, Catholics and liberals, this must be good.'

**Answer:** This line of thinking rests on the idea that the end justifies the means. If it seems to work, it must be right. Results count more than the purity of the methods we use. This is the reasoning of an ungodly and immoral age, and it often taints the thinking of Christian people. Therefore, if an evangelist appears to be winning souls, then it is assumed that God must be with him, and whether or not he compromises with non-evangelicals does not matter – he must be right.

However, the Bible condemns the attitude which says – 'Let us do evil, that good may come' *(Romans 3.8)*. Christians must never ignore the rules of the Bible because compromise *seems* to lead to success. The Lord, by His grace, sometimes continues to use His people (at least for a time) even though they do wrong and grieve Him, but they still have a duty to conform their methods to His Word. Christians should never take advantage of God's patience towards them by interpreting it as a licence for them to do as they please. We have several biblical examples of this.

Moses, for example, disobeyed God when he struck the rock (on the second occasion) to secure water for the congregation *(Numbers 20.7-13)*. Despite his disobedience, God honoured him and water flowed. Nevertheless, Moses did wrong, and later had to pay for his disobedience. Blessing never absolves us from the duties of self-examination, obedience, and reform. (See, for example, *Romans 6.1-2* and *Hebrews 3.7-10*.)

God reproves His people – 'that take counsel, but not of me; and that cover with a covering, but not of my spirit . . . that walk to go down into Egypt, and have not asked at my mouth; to strengthen themselves in the strength of Pharaoh, and to trust in the shadow of Egypt . . . Woe to them that go down to Egypt for help' *(Isaiah 30.1-2; 31.1)*. Obedience is paramount in the Christian life. The Lord loves obedience better than sacrifice. 'If ye love me, keep my commandments,' says the Lord *(John 14.15)*. The apostle John says: 'Let us not love in word, neither in tongue; but in deed and in truth' *(1 John 3.18)*.

The Bible gives very definite rules both in the matter of who we fellowship with, and who we co-operate with in His work. God does not want crowds to be gathered (or other things to be achieved) with the help of His enemies. He does not need the co-operation of Catholics and theological liberals. He calls His people to work independently of all false teachers, and in dependence upon His mighty power.

## *(2) The Lord Jesus Christ never separated from false teachers*

'It is permissible to co-operate and fellowship with those who do not share our evangelical views because Jesus did so. He accepted the invitations of the Pharisees and Jewish leaders when He spoke in the Temple and the synagogues, and He never separated Himself from them.'

**Answer:** This argument is so contrary to the sheer weight of facts that it is surprising to hear it so often used. The Lord had a duty to go into the Temple and the synagogues, partly because He lived a life of obedience under the law, and partly because He was the rightful King and Lord of the people. However, whenever He was in those places He boldly exposed and opposed the religious leaders, with the result that He provoked their constant hostility, and their attempts against His life. Everyone in Israel in those days could see the great gulf between the Lord and the Jewish leaders! Compare the conduct of the Lord with that of ecumenical evangelicals today. When the Saviour visited the Temple, did He embrace the unbelieving

Pharisees and pray with them? Did He give a public impression of spiritual approval, or exchange cordial greetings? Did He work with them on committees and joint endeavours? Did He discuss with them how His doctrine and theirs might be reconciled? Of course not.

The fact is that He publicly condemned most of those Jewish teachers as blind and self-righteous hypocrites, even calling them a generation of vipers. He accused them of shutting the people out of the kingdom of Heaven, and He made clear that they were shut out themselves. He called their prayers a pretence and condemned their religious practices. He said that they were the destroyers of God's true message and (unless they repented) would not escape the damnation of hell. All this is to be found in *Matthew 23.13-33*. In one discourse the Lord pronounced no fewer than eight woes upon the Jewish leaders in the full hearing of the multitude. In numerous other discourses He said similar things.

The entire public ministry of the Lord Jesus was opposed to the false teaching of the Jewish leaders, and this (humanly speaking) was the basis of their hatred of Him, leading to the cross of Calvary. In almost every public address, the Saviour made some statement to dissociate Himself from the Jewish leaders, the scribes and the Pharisees. No serious reader of the Gospels can fail to see the Lord's condemnation of false teachers on almost every visit to the Temple and the synagogues. All but one of the Lord's Temple visits resulted in a confrontation with the Jews, and twice they tried to take His life. The synagogue visits also produced hostility and antagonism, with two more attempts upon His life.

Does the Lord's stance toward false teachers bear any resemblance to the conduct of present-day ecumenical evangelicals when they associate with non-evangelicals? Ecumenical evangelicals do the *exact opposite* of all that the Saviour did. To say that the Lord never separated from the false teachers of His day is almost ludicrous, for He verbally separated Himself from them virtually every day of His earthly ministry.

## (3) The Corinthians and Galatians were never told to separate

'Paul never told the sound members of the church at Corinth to resign their membership even though their church was full of great problems. Nor did Paul counsel the sound believers in the churches of Galatia to leave, even though these churches had virtually forsaken the faith.'

**Answer:** This argument is mistaken for two reasons. First, the churches mentioned were not 'false', but only tainted by false ideas. Secondly, the members of both churches *were* taught separation, for they were ordered to expel the minority of wayward people in each case. Take first the church at Corinth. Despite its defects, it was not overrun by fundamental doctrinal heresy. Its problems were capable of being corrected. The most serious problem was the toleration of a moral offender. The apostle did not counsel resignation from the church for the simple reason that he commanded them to put out that guilty member. He therefore did teach separation, but by the expulsion of the offender rather than by the resignation of the majority.

In *1 Corinthians 5.9-11* (as we have noted earlier), Paul teaches the duty of expulsion (a form of separation) for a whole range of offences. He tells the Corinthians that they must separate from professing Christians who commit these offences. They must separate from fornicators, covetous people, idolaters (ie: religious compromisers), slanderers, drunkards and swindlers. Furthermore they must shun such offenders at a *social* level also by not eating with them.

In his second letter to the Corinthians Paul gives another powerful command to separate from false religion – the one most often quoted – in *2 Corinthians 6.14-18*. The Corinthian letters are so full of instruction about separation that it is utterly bewildering to find them used as a justification for non-separation!

What about the churches of Galatia? Is it correct to say they were not counselled to separate from false teaching? It is not correct. Paul knew very well that the members of these churches were mostly converted people who had been visited and disturbed by false teachers. His task was to remonstrate with them, and to urge them to keep to the Truth. At the same time he commanded them to have nothing further to do with those false teachers. In other words, he *did* press upon them the duty of separation. In *Galatians 1.8-9* he clearly stated that false teachers must be *accursed* (excommunicated). In *Galatians 5.12* he reinforced this, saying that false teachers should be *cut off*, which literally means 'amputated'. He denounced such teachers in the strongest terms.

The commands to separate from error in the Corinthian and Galatian epistles could not be more emphatic. In the light of this, we cannot understand how the opponents of biblical separation find justification for their position in these epistles. Their arguments can hardly be regarded as credible.

## *(4) The prophets of old stayed within wayward communities*

'Separation is wrong because the prophets of old were called to stay and minister within Israel even though that nation was disobedient and far from God. Their example shows that one can preach against the error of a community while remaining within it.'

**Answer:** This argument is as surprising as the previous one, for the prophets could not have been more independent of the religious establishment than they were, nor could they have more clearly dissociated themselves from wicked leaders and false teachers.

In Old Testament times God certainly called them to remain within Israel. But much of their message was to warn Israel that God would soon end this arrangement because it was offensive to Him. (See, for example, *Jeremiah 31.31-34.*) The prophets predicted that in New Testament times the true Church would be separated from the nation of Israel. Ecumenical evangelicals today seem to be trying to put the clock back to Old Testament times.

It must be emphasised that the prophets never co-operated with false teachers. While, by God's command for that time, they stayed within Israel, they denounced idol-worship and set themselves against evil kings. We may think of Elijah, Jeremiah and Ezekiel and the hostility and suffering they incurred for their 'separate' stand. All the prophets of old stood against the prevailing evils of the religious establishment and suffered the consequences. None of them made peace with ungodly leaders, nor with the prophets of Baal. The idea that they had spiritual fellowship with such people, or that they co-operated in any way, cannot be regarded as serious exposition of the Bible.

## (5) The Bible makes belief in Christ's deity the only condition for fellowship

'The Bible authorises separation only when the deity of Christ is denied. *2 John 7* defines a false teacher as someone who denies that Jesus Christ came in the flesh. All who acknowledge that Jesus Christ has come in the flesh are acceptable for fellowship and co-operation irrespective of their views on other doctrines.'

**Answer:** Although we have already considered this line of reasoning, we will expand a little on this point as this is the chief argument used in favour of ecumenism at the present time. This application of *2 John 7* is mistaken because it takes a most superficial view of the text, ignoring the clear implication of John's words. The text reads: 'For many deceivers are entered into the world, who confess not that Jesus Christ is come in the flesh. This is a deceiver and an antichrist.'

John's statement is to be taken *seriously* and *logically*. What does acceptance of Christ's deity *imply*? If a person *really* believes that a member of the Godhead came to Earth in the flesh he will inevitably believe the *consequences* of that. He will believe that every word of Christ's was infallible, and to be obeyed. He will believe in His sinlessness, His power, His miracles, and in His own explanation of His mission.

How could anyone *truly* believe that Christ was God, and at the same time believe Him to be mistaken in the things He said and did? If a theological liberal denies the infallibility of Christ's words, disbelieves the resurrection and miracles, and rejects Christ's atonement, we must not accept his claim that he believes that Christ was God. It is a glib and empty claim. It is a meaningless claim. It is not consistent with his critical spirit toward Christ, and his rejection of His teaching. His claim is mere words.

Indeed, we do not need to ask his views on the deity of Christ, because his unbelief in other vital doctrines speaks louder than his words. He cannot seriously and truly believe that God has come in the flesh, because he has insufficient respect for Him, and therefore we must not extend spiritual recognition and approval to that liberal.

If we take a still closer look at what John says, we note that he gives the Lord His *title*, as well as His personal name. He condemns all those teachers 'who confess not that Jesus CHRIST is come in the flesh'. The term *Christ*, or *anointed one*, indicates God's appointed *Messiah*, Who would save people from sin. Every time the word *Christ* is mentioned it is like the ringing of a beautiful bell which reminds us of the Saviour's finished work on Calvary, and of the glorious doctrine of justification by grace, through faith.

John defines a false teacher as one who does not believe that God's appointed sin-bearer, the perfect propitiation for all our sins, has come. He says, in effect, that anyone who claims to be a Christian but does not believe that Christ on Calvary made a *full satisfaction* for sin, and that His work is the *sole ground* for the forgiveness of all sins, is a deceiver.

We remember that the official position of the Roman Catholic Church is utterly to condemn such teaching. Catholic doctrine flatly contradicts the sole sufficiency of the merits of Christ, and justification by faith alone. But this is the doctrine that John insists upon. John does not mean his words to be taken as a mere technicality. He provides an efficient and adequate test of a person's belief. He means us to ask the question, 'Do you believe that the infallible, miracle-working Son of God came to suffer and die on Calvary to bear away our sins and to be our only Priest and Mediator? Do you believe that by trusting in Him alone (and not to yourself or your church or any sacraments) your sins will be freely washed away and your soul saved?'

If a person cannot answer this kind of question affirmatively, then it is our task to show him, as warmly and tenderly as we can, the way of salvation, but not to extend recognition and fellowship to him as a saved person. It is our duty to show people the *full implications* of our Lord's deity, not to seal them in the darkness and delusion of a false form of Christianity.

John's test-question has been turned into a slick, superficial question shorn of its implications. This is the technique adopted by many evangelicals in order to justify their compromising ways in co-operating with false teachers.

The apostle John, two verses later, says, 'Whosoever... abideth not in the doctrine of Christ, hath not God.' He refers to the doctrine that Christ came in the flesh, suffered and died for sinners on Calvary, and became the perfect, all-sufficient Mediator and Saviour for those who come to God by Him. The doctrine of Christ includes all the Truth about His sinless person, His infallible teaching, and the authority of all His utterances. John says that if a teacher rejects the doctrine of Christ he is not to be regarded as a true Christian, and the people are to be warned that he is a false teacher. Co-operation with non-evangelicals is contrary to the Bible and deeply grievous to God. The use which ecumenical evangelicals have made of *2 John 7-9* is a travesty of the serious and honest exegesis of God's Word.

## (6) *Separation is the sin of schism*

'Separation is wrong because it is the sin of schism condemned in *1 Corinthians 1.10*, where Paul commands "that there be no divisions among you". Under no circumstances may we divide the Church of God.'

**Answer:** The first reply to this argument is simply to complete the quotation from *1 Corinthians 1.10*, where Paul says, 'Now I beseech you ... that ye all speak the same thing, and that there be no divisions among you; but that ye be perfectly joined together in the same mind and in the same judgment.'

The question must be asked – was the apostle 'perfectly joined together' in mind and judgement with the Judaisers, or with other unbelieving false teachers? It is obvious that the Holy Spirit (speaking through Paul) calls for unity between those who *can* be joined in mind and judgement, because they love and believe the same Gospel. It is foolish and wrong to apply the verse to promote unity with false teachers, for we are commanded *not* to agree with them!

Schism is a term which covers any form of division which is unjustified, such as that which is caused by petty strife, bad temper, an unforgiving spirit, self-seeking, pride, jealousy, factiousness, or lack of love. Any separation which is made in obedience to the clear command of Scripture (because of opposition to false doctrine or some other serious error) cannot possibly be the sin of schism.

## (7) *The wheat and tares must grow together*

'It is our duty to stay in denominations no matter how bad they become, and also to co-operate in our evangelism with those who do not share evangelical views, because the Lord tells us that His Church is bound to contain good and bad elements until the day of judgement. The parable of the wheat and tares tells us not to attempt to build a pure Church, but to let both grow together until the harvest.'

**Answer:** Those who use this argument in favour of non-separation from error do not take account of the Lord's own interpretation of His parable. They seem to think that the *field* in which the wheat and tares grow together represents the *Church*. They therefore conclude that the parable is talking about the Church when it says that Christians and unsaved people will exist together until the harvest.

However the Lord tells us in *Matthew 13.38* that the field

represents the *world*, not the Church! The parable does not speak about the Church at all. This elementary mistake in interpreting the parable has led to teaching which contradicts numerous New Testament passages. Verse after verse calls us to watch for false teaching, to keep it out of our congregations, and to reject those who are responsible for it. It is not the Lord's will that sound doctrine should grow alongside doctrines of demons in His Church until the end of time!

## (8) The Lord prayed for unity between Christians, not separation

'It is right to work with other professing Christians whether evangelical or not because the Lord prayed for such unity in *John 17.21*. He prayed – "That they all may be one ... that the world may believe that thou hast sent me." Separation always divides, and is therefore the opposite of what the Saviour desires and prays for.'

**Answer:** To understand Christ's words we must know exactly *who* were the people for whom He prayed. Did He pray for all people in the history of the world who merely *claimed* to be His followers? Or did He pray for true Christians? Clearly, He did not pray for false Christians, for He said, 'Many will say to me in that day, Lord, Lord, have we not prophesied in thy name ... and in thy name done many wonderful works? And then will I profess unto them, I never knew you: depart from me, ye that work iniquity' *(Matthew 7.22-23)*.

In *John 17* the Lord prayed exclusively for true Christians. When we read His prayer we find that He prayed for those who have eternal life and who know God (v 3); those who have come to Christ and keep His Word (v 6); those who have received the Truth (vv 7-8); those who are not of the world (vv 14 and 16); those who are one with the Godhead (v 21); those who have tasted the glory of God (v 22); those who are indwelt by Christ (v 23); those who are definitely going to Heaven (v 24); and those who have the joy of the Lord in them (v 26).

In other words, the Lord made it abundantly plain that His great prayer was *exclusively* for born-again people who know and love Him, and implicitly believe His Word. The Lord definitely did not pray this prayer for theological liberals; for those who deny vital doctrines, or reject justification by faith, or promote justification by works. Indeed, the unity for which Christ prayed is a unity which can exist only between true believers, because it is a unity in which His people are one in the same way that the Father, Son and Holy Spirit are one – 'that they may be one, even as we are one' (v 22). The members of the Godhead are united in *the Truth* and in *spiritual life*. The members of the glorious Godhead could never be found believing or saying different things!

As evangelical Christians we may be truly united spiritually only with those who share the Truth, and who share in that spiritual life which comes through conversion. We must never pretend that there is any spiritual unity between ourselves and those who have not found Christ, or who deny His Gospel.

## *(9) The Lord told us never to judge one another*

'We cannot separate from other professing Christians because the Lord said that we must not judge others. Those who are separatists possess a fault-finding spirit and condemn others in a way which the Saviour forbad when He said, "Judge not, that ye be not judged" *(Matthew 7.1).*'

**Answer:** Those who advance this argument take no account of the many scriptures which command us to exercise discernment in order to guard against false teachers. For example, *1 John 4.1* reads, 'Beloved, believe not every spirit, but try the spirits whether they are of God: because many false prophets are gone out into the world.' Also, *Romans 16.17* reads, 'Now I beseech you, brethren, mark them which cause divisions and offences contrary to the doctrine which ye have learned; and avoid them.'

It should be obvious that in *Matthew 7* the Lord is talking about *hypocritical* fault-finding. He particularly focuses on people who criticise others for doing things which they themselves do, and fail to consider the beam in their own eye. He does not speak against the duty of exercising discernment.

Those who think that in *Matthew 7.1* the Lord speaks against Christian discernment should read on to verses 15-23 of the same chapter. In verse 15 the Lord commands us to beware of false prophets who come to us in sheep's clothing but who are really wolves. Wolves must never be allowed to get among the sheep. But how shall we recognise wolves disguised as sheep without exercising discernment? He then says that we shall discern false teachers by their fruits, thus giving guidance as to *how* we may detect those who are to be rejected. Theological liberals publish much 'fruit' in the form of books which deny the faith. The 'fruit' of Roman Catholicism is the blasphemy of the Mass, and a host of other unbiblical practices.

In *Matthew 7.21-23* the Lord warns about many who claim to do wonderful things in His name, but they are workers of iniquity and He has nothing whatsoever to do with them. *He* did not fellowship with false workers, and He is our example.

If only those who use the argument quoted above would read the whole of *Matthew 7*, they would find that they have completely misapplied the Saviour's words, making Him teach the very opposite of all that He says throughout the remainder of the chapter.

## *(10) The Lord says, 'Strengthen the things which remain'*

'*Revelation 3.2* tells us to stay in our denominations regardless of the decadent theological views of the majority of ministers and churches in them. Our task is to uphold the Truth in the darkest places, and thus to "strengthen the things which remain". These words were addressed to Sardis, which was a dead church.'

**Answer:** Those who advance this argument assume too much in saying that the church at Sardis was entirely dead. For one thing, the church at Sardis appears to have been entirely orthodox in its beliefs.

It had not denied the fundamental, soul-saving doctrines of the faith. It enjoyed a reputation for theoretical soundness. Sardis was not told to discipline heretics and reform its doctrinal position; it was told, 'Wake up!' Sardis was reproved because the congregation, though nominally sound, was dead in terms of spiritual life and vitality. The people were sound, but sound asleep. The command – 'Strengthen the things which remain' – means: 'Stir the dying embers of spiritual life; preach the Gospel and walk with the Lord. End your cold formalism and backsliding!' The church at Sardis possessed the *Truth*, but needed *life*.

It is significant that the church at Sardis was given only a short time to repent and become a truly committed, earnest congregation. This hardly gives encouragement to evangelicals who spend their entire lives associating with non-evangelicals, who are both dead and unsound.

The letters to other churches in *Revelation 2-3* show that the Lord demands that false doctrine is given immediate corrective attention. Churches are severely reproved for tolerating false teachers for *any* length of time! Is this consistent with the idea that believers should remain in an apostate environment? The phrase addressed to Sardis in *Revelation 3.2* – 'Strengthen the things which remain' – was never intended as a justification of compromise. To pluck this verse out of context and to use it for this purpose involves tip-toeing through a minefield of neighbouring verses, all of which proclaim God's sternest disapproval of a doctrinally confused situation in His churches.

## *Stand for the Truth! A conclusion*

Any reader who evaluates the arguments *against* separation with a reasonable and fair mind will soon conclude that these constitute an alarmingly weak and ill-considered case. When able and gifted ministers are compelled to resort to arguments like these, the bankruptcy of ecumenism and inclusivism is obvious. Our clear biblical duty is to stand apart from, to remain separate from, all forms of false teaching, and to maintain a distinctive Gospel witness to the glory of God and the eternal salvation of precious souls. *This*, as we noted earlier, is the stand taken by our evangelical forbears. *This* is the attitude of orthodox, traditional evangelicalism. What we are seeing today is a new and radical departure from true evangelicalism. Where will we stand?